MISCONCEPTIONS ON HEALTH

FACTS ON DIETARY HABITS

GEETA GUPTA

Contents

Contents

Preface

I am involved with natural science out of curiosity to know what it is, how it works, and the logic behind this science. To know how we can treat different diseases by just changing our diet and lifestyle. Is it worth it?

I started to explore naturopathy and found that the yoga and Ayurvedic concepts are deeply related to our life and we are following them and getting the benefits too, without any awareness. This inspired me and I did a three-and-a-half-year entire course in Naturopathy and started my practice as a naturopath. I further studied different acupressure therapies too and came to know about Guasa therapy, a 5000 years old therapy that gives effective and quick results but still we are not familiar with it. I studied it deeply and got enormous results through my practice.

During my practice as a Naturopath, I got attached to a well-known nutraceutical company and treated various patients through natural remedies. At my clinic, I treat people with diet, nutrients, and different therapies. I am thankful to God for choosing me as a medium to serve people by giving health awareness. I also want to thank my parents, family, and friends for their unconditional blessings and support.

Disclaimer

The information provided in this book is for general awareness purposes only. This book does not harm any religion, race, caste, creed, colour, or gender. This book is only for information purposes.

Food

Our body needs food to survive but all foods don't affect our health equally. That is why it is said that we are what we eat. However, it can be tough to eat right, all the time. But the accurate knowledge about food products and their nutrients may help us to plan the proper diet and maintain a fit body.

There is enormous information regarding food all around us, it's hard to know what's true and what's not. Even though dieticians, doctors, and health practitioners guide us on the right way to eat, somehow we don't get their usage instructions and get stuck in the grip of false notions.

So, to get rid of these myths, read the following facts to clear up confusion about nutrition. Maybe this information helps us to make necessary changes in our daily eating patterns.

CHAPTER ONE

Food can affect Hormonal Balance

We all know that everything we consume leaves a specific impact on our bodies. Different food products affect us differently depending on the various components and their properties. So what kind of food we have and in what quantity always matter. We might not be aware that certain foods can be responsible for hormonal imbalance in our bodies. That is why, proper awareness about food products is, essential for us to get perfect health. Let's disclose them!

- **Soy food:** It might be surprising for us that the soya foods which we generally considered a healthy food option, can be the cause of hormonal imbalance. The reason is that soya food contains a bioactive substance called phytoestrogen, which acts like estrogen in the body. When we consume soy in excess, it contradicts natural estrogen hormones. Our body gets confused by thinking that there is a sufficient supply of estrogen and it reduces the production of real estrogen. Thereby if we eat soya products regularly, then over time it can create an adverse impact on our health.

- **Red meat:** Excessive eating of red meat can also increase the production of estrogen in the body. That is why it should be avoided to eat daily.

- **Caffeine:** If we consume it several times a day, it can increase the cortisol hormone production in the body which can bring our body into alert mode, which can increase our craving for food. That is why it is preferred to take such foods in limited quantities.

- **Processed food:** Mostly processed foods contain preservatives, sodium, sugar syrups, etc. This dangerous combination stresses the adrenal glands and puts you at the risk of hormonal imbalances. Even frequent drinking of energy drinks and overeating sugary food products like sweets, chocolates, and candies can cause hormonal imbalance.

- **Stevia:** No doubt, stevia is a good substitute for refined sugar but excess intake of it can create adverse effects on fertility or monthly cycles. So, if you are pregnant or suffering from any hormonal issue, you should not consume. Even certain vegetables like broccoli, kale, brinjal, and tomato should not be consumed in excess as they can disturb the thyroid gland's functions.

In such a way, these certain foods can disturb our body's hormonal balance, thereby if we want to steer clear of hormonal issues we need to limit them in our diet.

CHAPTER TWO

Healthy food can be unhealthy

Numerous misconceptions get perpetuated about different foods but many times they are just rumours, the facts are quite different. Quite a few food products are considered healthy in general and are consumed without proper guidance. These do not just affect the health of our body even creating certain ailments. As some healthy foods can't be consumed in excess, sometimes we couldn't even combine two very healthy food products. They can create serious health complications. For example: according to Ayurveda, we should not consume desi ghee(clarified butter) and honey together in equal quantities, as it will become toxic and, eventually destroy our immunity (however both are highly nutritious).

Likewise, there is plenty of nutritious misinformation about food products. These are necessary to be cleared out for the sake of sound health. Let's dive in.

- **Apple cider vinegar** is good for overall health but just knowing its benefits, if we intake vinegar regularly it can deplete potassium in the body and can create hypokalaemia. Also, excess use of vinegar can weaken the bones. It can even enhance the acidity problem. So for the safe side, we should avoid consuming it regularly.

- **Coconut oil** also has several health benefits and healing qualities. But it is not suitable for all as it contains about 90% saturated fat, which is a higher percentage than butter (about 64% saturated fat). So, it is better to avoid using it regularly.

- We often believe that **canned and frozen foods** have preservatives in them and contain fewer nutrients than fresh fruits and vegetables. But here we should not forget that some preservatives are also used in fresh fruits and vegetables which can affect their nutritious value too.
  Secondly, more often fresh fruits or vegetables have had a long journey from the fields to the vegetable market. Sometimes, it takes weeks to reach their destination (customer). During the journey, enzymes are released in them and they lose some nutrients. Instead of this, canned or frozen fruits and vegetables are processed in a way that their nutrients get locked in, and surprisingly, it is found that some canned and frozen foods have more nutrients than fresh ones.

- We generally think that **brown sugar** is better than white sugar so we should prefer to use it for gaining optimal health benefits but the fact is not the same, because the only difference between brown and white sugar is the process, in which both are going through.
  Brown sugar contains white sugar with molasses, which has a caramel aroma and flavour, whereas white sugar has been refined to remove the molasses. But both of these sugars contain almost the same amount of calories as one teaspoon of brown sugar provides -15 calories, while the same amount of white sugar provides -16.3 calories. Aside from these minor differences, they are nutritionally similar.

- Equivalently, most people perceive that **brown eggs** are healthier than white eggs. No doubt brown and white eggs taste different but it is also a fact that there is no nutritional difference between them. However brown eggs are more expensive than white eggs but just because of the difference in the hens that lay them as brown eggs are laid by red-feathered chickens having large body sizes and requiring more feed, thereby the cost of brown eggs is increased and they are more expensive than white eggs.

- Most people avoid consuming eggs because they think that eggs can increase the **cholesterol** level in the body. Of course, eggs surely do contain cholesterol but it is also true that they are not the only factor that is responsible for high blood cholesterol or cardiovascular disease in healthy individuals.
  The reason is, that we might get only 25% cholesterol directly from food. The rest is synthesized by the liver when we eat other sources of saturated fat like butter, oil, ghee, etc.
  Eggs have plenty of other nutrients that even offset the negative effects of cholesterol as egg yolks are rich in choline which is essential for muscle function. That is why fitness experts recommend that one yolk egg or two egg whites can be consumed daily.

- More often we prefer to eat **fat-free foods** to maintain good health. But we are unaware that these fat-free foods generally go through a process that removes a lot of nutritional fat. Thus they may not contain nutrients up to the mark. So it is better that, before adopting any fat-free food first we should check the nutrition label to see how many calories are in one serving and the nutritious value they contain so that we can select them as per our requirements.

- We think that if a particular food does not contain sugar, it must be healthier for us. The fact is, in such **sugar-free** foods, the sugar is removed but more often it is replaced with harmful chemicals, which can create some other complications regarding health. Therefore, we should always be conscious of ingredients before consuming these foods.

- **Artificial sweeteners** are generally considered safe, some people can be sensitive to these sweeteners and experience symptoms such as headache, bloating and upset stomach, etc. so we should not use them blindly. This means to say, the food products that we believe may give more health benefits, unknowingly can create more health complications.

- These days **alkaline water** is very popular for providing myriad health benefits which we can't deny but we should also be aware that if it is taken in excess, it can create gastrointestinal issues and skin irritations. Similarly, if it is taken before a meal, it will neutralize the acidity level in the stomach, resulting in food not being digested properly. So, before drinking it, it is better to acquire proper knowledge about when and how much alkaline water we can consume.

- We should not limit ourselves to drinking 8 glasses of **water** daily because we can't decide what particular amount of water we need daily as basic hydration varies for each individual's body tendency. It depends on various factors like our exercise and activity level, weather, health problems, age, etc. It also depends on what kind of food we eat (as if we eat more carbs, our body needs less water). Thus, we can't bind ourselves to drink 8 glasses of water daily.
  So the thumb rule can be, drink water when you are thirsty, no need to count the glasses.

On the whole, we can say that nutrition misinformation is everywhere. Our health is dependent on how conscious we are. Only through our awareness can food products provide wellness appropriately.

CHAPTER THREE

Spicy food can cause Ulcers or Inflammation

Undoubtedly, spices play a significant role in food. Every spice has its flavouring and essence that make the food healthy and tasty. Also, these spices are a rich source of vitamins, minerals, and other beneficial substances. Even they prevent several diseases by fighting free radicals and increasing the body's immunity.

Indian food is mostly known for its tempting varieties and spicy flavours. But unfortunately, we assume that these spices can form ulcers in the stomach because of their hot tendency. But the fact is quite different. Let's know in detail.

The fact is that most Indian foods are prepared on the basic principle of Ayurveda which believes that a balanced diet contains six tastes; sweet, sour, salty, bitter, pungent, and astringent. Each taste has a specific energetic effect on the body. They can warm us or cool us down. Taken together in appropriate amounts, the six tastes can create a sense of real satisfaction.

Thereby, from ancient times, Indian food contains spices. These spices are like 'herbal medicine' as they contain different tastes which our body needs, they not only fill up our temptation but also nourish our body. Anyhow some spices have a hot tendency but that doesn't mean they are 'spicy hot' as they are neutralized with other cool tendencies containing herbs, for example, if most Indian foods contain chilly, carom on the other side they also contain cumin seeds, fennel seeds, etc. Thus, these spices are very effective for the proper digestion process but still do not harm the bodily tissue if they are consumed in the right quantity.

Besides this, usually, ulcers are caused by the bacteria Helicobacter Pylori, even sometimes ulcers can be caused by some medications or due to excessive acid in the stomach. So these spices are not the culprit to form ulcers. But yes, if the ulcer is formed, spicy food can irritate it and can cause severe pain in the stomach.

To get rid of these health complications, Ayurveda gives a lot of great information about healthy eating and guides us on what amount of specific spices we can include in our diet according to one's constitution, health issues, region, and season that they can provide us enormous health benefits.

CHAPTER FOUR

Reduction of Fat products isn't always healthy

Dietary fat is one of the most confusing food topics around. They are not as bad as we consider. It is a source of essential fatty acids, which the body cannot make itself so we need fat to survive and it serves many vital functions. Thus, they are essential for good health. How is it done, let's find out!

Fats are an important part of our diet as they are essential for absorbing some nutrients such as carotenoids (the pigments that produce bright colour in plants) and vitamins A, E, D, and K by dissolving them. We all know that some fats are required for basic functions in the body such as cellular development and the nervous system as they provide essential nutrients and most importantly Omega-3 and omega 6. These fatty acids can help to lower the amount of bad cholesterol in the blood.

We should include healthy fats (monounsaturated fats and polyunsaturated fats) in our diet, found in – seeds, olives, avocados, sunflowers, soya bean oil and canola oil etc. Most nuts also contain healthy fats as they are a good source of protein, dietary fibre and minerals including magnesium, zinc, copper, etc. Therefore, we should add it up to our meal as a one-half ounce of mixed nuts which has about only 100 calories. If we soak them in water and then consume them, they can be more beneficial for our health.

We should include Desi ghee in our diet (in small quantity) because it contains CLA (conjugated linoleic acid) which helps to mobilize the stubborn fat in the body. According to Ayurveda, we should consume pure, cow ghee approximate ½ teaspoon daily. There is no harm, but it should be *Desi* (Indian) Cow's homemade Ghee (clarified butter).

Overall we can say that we don't have to cut all fat out of our diet. However, we can limit the amount of fat we eat. The most important thing is, that the type of fat and how we involve it in our dietary routine makes the whole difference.

CHAPTER FIVE

Misconceptions about Food

Many people have plenty of misinterpretations that the food which they consider as healthy and nutritious food, most probably may not be as nutritious as they believe. Likewise, sometimes they are under the impression that the particular food might harm their health, but the fact is a little bit different. There are numerous notions regarding food products around us, the need is that we should be more aware of the real facts. Let's know about them one by one.

Most of us believe that eating carrots daily helps to improve our eyes but the fact is quite different from it. Vitamin A is essential for good eye health. Since carrots are rich in beta carotene (an orange pigment) that our body can convert into vitamin A. Therefore it is believed that carrots are very beneficial for eye health but if we eat more than required, it doesn't mean that they will improve eyesight. Even other sources of Vitamin A containing food such as mango, banana, papaya, turmeric, apricot, etc. are also beneficial for eye health.

Virtually, it is often said that some foods contain zero calories. But the fact is that no food has zero calories, all foods contain some calories. But yes, some foods have fewer calories such as cucumber, onion, celery, lettuce, and some citrus fruits as they contain a lot of water and fibre in them. As we know that when we chew and digest food, our body burns some calories. When we gain calories from food as much as the body needs to digest them, such foods are called zero calories foods.

Milk is often considered a complete food but the fact is, it contains approximately 87% water. The nutrients like protein, carbohydrates, vitamins, and minerals are all found in the other 13%. If we consume low-fat milk and skimmed milk these nutrients are also reduced. Thus, milk is a nutritious food but not complete food. Also, if we consume in excess it can lead to increased sebum production which can cause aches and other skin problems.

Furthermore, we generally believe that dairy products are essential for strong bones but only calcium is and we can get calcium from different sources too like seafood, leafy green (broccoli, cabbage) legumes, tofu, dried fruit (almond, figs), seeds (poppy, sesame seeds) and various food that are fortified with calcium. But here we should consider that although some vegetables such as spinach and rhubarb are good sources of calcium, it is seen that they are also high in oxalates which decrease calcium absorption.

Similarly, most people think that rice is the cause of fattening but we should not forget that rice is high in carbohydrates but not high in fat. When taken in the right quantity and at the right time, it will be utilized by the body and we will not gain weight. We know that a large number of people prefer to eat rice instead of wheat, but they all are not obese. Therefore, rice is not the only factor in weight gain.

Mango, Grapes, and bananas are also considered weight gain culprits and enemies for diabetics. But we should not forget that they are highly nutritious foods, however, they contain a rich amount of natural sugar content but if these foods can be consumed at the right time and in the right quantity may not be harmful to us. Even if we eat them in time and remain active, then they can surely provide fruitful benefits. For example - Mangoes have anti-inflammatory and antioxidant properties and are rich in fibre. When consumed in between meals, they give fullness. Bananas are also high in vitamin b6 and fibre and can be part of breakfast.

Thus, these fruits can be included in the diet, if we do a little extra workout so that they can digest properly and provide essential nutrients to the body.

On one hand, some food is underestimated for their properties, meanwhile, others are overrated. For example, it is believed that cranberry juice can cure urinary tract infections but the fact is, a urinary tract infection requires antibiotics to be cured. But yes, drinking cranberry juice may help to prevent UTIs from coming back but can't cure them individually.

Another common belief is that heat destroys enzymes in food. But it is not the ultimate truth because as a matter of fact, cooking breaks down fibre to the point where it can be easily digested. Moreover, even in some foods, cooking boosts the levels of nutrients. For example, ketchup contains a richer amount of lycopene (an antioxidant) than raw tomatoes. Cooking carrots also increases their nutritional value as boiling carrots leads to carotenoids (antioxidants) being increased by 14%. Therefore, if we consume boiled carrots rather than raw form, they would be more nutritious.

It is believed that microwave radiation destroys the nutrient content in food. But the fact is microwaves penetrate food and heat it more competently and quickly compared to other cooking methods. The nutrients also have less time to break down. It is important to note that all types of cooking tend to cause a loss of nutrients. The key to minimizing it is to keep the cooking time short. As the microwaves affect mainly water molecules, they steam food from inside out and thus, help to retain most nutrients.

On the whole, there are plenty of misconceptions about food Items, but we should always be aware of what food, how much food, and which form of food we can eat and get maximum benefits from them.

Surprisingly, we have many more misconceptions regarding food products that may never be noticed, but undoubtedly they are mesmerizing us. So we notice how the healthy things that hear in day-to-day life, might not be as they are said to be. As generations passed, we kept following the wrong norms without actually researching about them and carry forward these false facts to the next generation, unknowingly.

CHAPTER SIX

Interesting facts about Food

This chapter contains interesting yet useful facts about various fruits, vegetables, dry fruits etc. These facts are helpful to clear misconceptions and help you in your understanding of various factors around us which can affect our health. It will help you improve your diet even further.

- **Figs are fruit?** Figs are not a fruit, but rather they are inverted flowers and their seeds are pollinated by tiny wasps.

- **Walnuts are nuts?** Technically, they are not nuts but rather "seeds of drupes.'

- **Peanuts are nuts?** Most edible nuts grow on trees, but Peanuts grow in pods that mature underground like legumes. So botanically, peanuts belong to the family of legumes.

- **Feeding the gut bacteria:** Just like the body's cells, the gut bacteria (collectively called microbiota) need to eat and the soluble fibre is their preferred fuel source. This may be the most important reason to include plenty of fibre in our diet to feed the beneficial bacteria in our intestines.

- **Food Craving:** Have you ever noticed that when you overeat sugary foods, you crave more of them? That's because an overload of sugar spikes dopamine levels and leaves you wanting more.

- **Drinking tea or coffee with meals** makes it harder for the body to absorb iron from plant food. So, avoid these beverages at meal time.

- **Obese people can be malnourished** if they eat too many fatty foods or empty-calorie foods that can create a deficiency of vitamins and minerals in the body.

- **Apples can float** in water because they are 25% airy.

- **Honey:** Bees are not the only ones with the skills to produce honey, Mexican honey wasps too can make delicious honey. Honey doesn't expire when it is properly stored in sealed containers. It can remain stable for centuries. It is believed that honey with ghee mixed in equal quantity becomes poison.

- **Potatoes are poisonous?** Green potatoes are one of the most common reasons for solanine poisoning.

- **Spices:** Spices contain natural preservatives. So if you season the food, it will last longer. Spices speed up digestion, when you eat spicy food your saliva secretion increases and this speeds up digestion.

- **Pumpkins** are usually labelled as vegetables but they are technically a fruit because it is believed that anything that starts from a flower is botanically a fruit.

- Almost all **yellow-coloured fruits** and vegetables contain vitamin A.

- **Milk-based products** (milk, yoghurt, cream, ice cream) are the best reliever of spiciness. The reason is that they contain a protein called Casein. This fat-living molecule binds to the capsaicin molecules (the spicy compound of chillies). They surround them and wash them away. That is why we feel relief.

- The **older egg will float** in the water. If it floats on top it is not good to eat.

- The **Cavendish banana is seedless** and can't reproduce, so every banana is a clone.

- **Strawberries are not true berries** because berries only have seeds on the inside and strawberry seeds are on the outside. They are classified as members of the rose family.

- **Expiry dates on Bottle water** Water can't expire but bottles can. Plastic bottles will eventually start leaking chemicals into the water. That is why we should always check the expiration date of water bottles before drinking the water.

- **Children eat what they like** – Children develop food taste according to what they eat regularly. So, it would be better to give them healthy food only.

- **Taste and Flavours:** Flavours are a combination of smell and taste perception. The aroma in food is perceived through gustation (through taste receptors in the mouth) Orthonasal-olfaction (smelling the food through the nose) and retronasal-olfaction (where the odour molecules travel through the back of your mouth and into the nose).
  That is why food tastes bland when we have a cold or a stuffy nose. Likewise, straws also inhibit our orthonasal and retronasal olfaction. This is the reason why we breathe out into the mouth after tasting something delicious, also it can enhance the overall

flavours.

In such a way, there are plenty of surprises which are concealed in nature that are revealed from time to time by different food organizations and researchers. Through their admirable work, we can perceive the secrets of mysterious nature.

Weight Loss

It's quite natural that everyone wants to maintain a healthy weight and remain slim and fit. But most of the time, even though we are doing everything right, we may not get desirable results. This is because, unknowingly, we make some negligible mistakes which become obstacles to achieving our goal to lose weight. Moreover, there are a lot of misconceptions regarding weight loss which create confusion in our minds. Doctors, Dieticians, and Health practitioners guide us and make us aware of the right way to lose weight, but most of the time we might not get their valuable advice. But, it's really important to clear out these misconceptions and know the facts, before adopting any weight loss programme. Let's discuss them one by one in detail.

CHAPTER SEVEN

Weight gain is not Fat gain

Probably we are confused between fat gain and weight gain and very often when we gain weight, we start trying to reduce fat in our body without knowing the real reason for weight gain, so we don't get desirable results although we put hard efforts to reduce it. We also need to understand that fat takes years to accumulate so we can't reduce it within a few days. These premises must be cleared out before we see the visual results of weight loss.

If we need to cure obesity, first of all, we must remain attentive to the fact that our weight gain is a fat gain or something else as weight gain (obesity) is a very complex disorder. Many genetic, biological and environmental factors can affect our body weight. Various medical conditions and some medicines can be responsible for weight gain. Numerous hormones are also supposed to regulate body weight. So, we can't consider that fat is the only culprit of weight gain. There are plenty of reasons for obesity that we can't ignore.

A second big mistake we make is when we often use weighing machines to keep watch on our weight fluctuations in gained weight. We assume that we are gaining more fat and thus start to put pressure on ourselves. We either reduce our diet conspicuously or overexert ourselves by doing intense exercises. But here we should not forget that the weighing scale measures overall body weight, not specifically fat content. Therefore, we can't rely on how much fat or muscles we have and in what amount. Even many times we just gain water weight instead of fat weight.

That is why we always remain aware that if we are on a strict low-calorie diet but notice that we have gained weight, it's likely to be water weight. This happens usually due to increased glycogen, which is stored in our muscles as fuel. This glycogen increases only when we intake excess sugar (glucose) in any form, like refined sugar, sweets, or even carbs (which contain sufficient water in them). Excess sodium intake can also be the cause of water weight. That is why when we put on weight, firstly, we should focus on our daily diet pattern. If we are consuming excess sugar-rich foods daily and then we should start to reduce them from our diet, gradually we find that we started to lose weight.

We should also be aware that, even sometimes hormonal changes in women can lead to greater water retention levels in the body that can be the major cause of weight gain. Therefore, we can't blame only fat for increasing our weight. Thereby we need regular check-ups to diagnose the correct reason for weight gain so that we can reduce the weight in the right way.

Another thing we should consider is that if we follow any diet plan and lose weight rapidly it may be water weight loss because the body decreases water weight first whereas fat remains the same. Losing fat is not so easy, it needs our regular passionate efforts, discipline in lifestyle, and patience for visual results.

Furthermore, most people think that if they lose weight, then their belly will be the first to get in shape. The fact is, when we lose fat, it reduces from all over the body and not just from any particular part of it. So when we lose weight, we can't be choosy, where we will start to reduce first. But yes, some yoga asanas are effective to reduce belly fat more quickly like triangle pose, bow pose, bridge pose, chair pose, etc.

No doubt, adopting the right lifestyle and diet plan may help you to lose weight but it is also true that the transition to a healthier lifestyle won't happen overnight. So if you want to lose fat appropriately, the first step should be managing your expectations and avoiding putting pressure on yourself.

CHAPTER EIGHT

Calorie intake is not the only factor

We generally believe that 'taking fewer calories and burning more' is the key to weight loss, but it is not the only thing that matters. Some other factors which we need to consider, are as follows:

- The type of food you eat matters much more than the number of calories it contains: both in terms of weight loss or weight gain. For example, glucose and fructose provide the same number of calories per gram but the body metabolizes them completely in different ways, as glucose can be metabolized by all of our body's tissues but fructose can only be metabolized by the liver.
- Similarly, some foods require more calories to digest, absorb and metabolize than others. For example, A high protein diet requires more calories to be metabolized than a carbohydrate-rich diet. Although, they have the same calorie content (as 1 gram of protein or carbs contains 4 calories).
- Like that, different types of food may also affect differently how full we feel, however they contain the same calories. For example – eating a 100-calories serving of oatmeal will reduce our hunger more effectively than eating a 100-calories serving of one chocolate candy. So, no need to concentrate only on the calorie value of foods.
- We should focus on the nutrient value of food products along with calories because if foods contain fewer calories and fewer

nutrients too, then they are not good for our overall health and may lead to fatigue, weak immunity, dizziness, and even fainting.

On the whole, we can say that we should not always remain conscious only of calorie intake. Besides, we should focus more on how nutritious our diets are. Thereby calorie counting is not the parameter for weight loss.

CHAPTER NINE

Are Diet plans effective?

Dieting is the practice of eating healthy food in a regulated way, but if we restrict ourselves from our favourite food, we start to feel more cravings for them. So most people get fed up with these restrictions and start eating more unhealthy food and regain the lost weight. But actually, we need not compromise this aspect. Just focus on the total calorie intake and limit excess eating. Even if we do extra workouts to burn, these extra calories then these high-calorie foods will not be obstacles to weight loss.

Also, the diet (as you think) doesn't need to be the best for you and surely gives miracle results because everyone has a different body type and health level. The same diet that works wonders for others, might not work for you. So while choosing the diet plan just consider all aspects because very often the diet which we contemplate as the perfect diet can be harmful to us. This means to say we must evaluate the diet plans before opting for the specific one, as we can gain optimal results from our passionate efforts toward weight loss.

- We generally perceive that fasting is a very effective way to lose weight, but the fact is that fasting is not as simple as it seems. Because when we do fast, we often experience that, it is difficult for us to focus on work with an empty stomach as it creates stress in the body and enhances our craving for tempting food and whenever we lose our willpower and attack our favourite food, we tend to consume more calories. This means to say, we can't lose weight, if we do fast and control our hunger all day, but cap it off with a huge meal that replaces all the calories we skipped earlier. As well as the persons who are suffering from diabetes or kidney disorders or anaemic can't do fasting for a long period.

- Similarly skipping meals is also not the ideal way to lose weight as it can create the adverse effects on the body, because when we don't eat for a long time, our body goes into 'survival mode' then metabolism gets slow and the body starts to conserve energy for an emergency, in result we feel fatigued and weakness in the body. In this state, our body starts to look out for other options. The easiest way is to use the muscle glycogen storage and we gradually start to lose muscle content and subsequently we lose body weight too. Thus, sometimes skipping meals can also be a cause of losing precious muscle content whereas our fat content remains the same.

- These days, fad diets are very popular for quick weight loss (Fad diet means, drinking blended juice for weeks to lose weight). But how much it is helpful for weight loss in a healthy manner, is questionable. Because it can also lead to adverse effects on the body as:
  Firstly, a fad diet may not provide all the nutrients (Protein, fat etc.) which our body needs.
  Secondly, it may increase the potassium level in the body. There is also a possible risk of an upset stomach if the juice is high in fructose (fruit sugar). However, we may lose weight initially due to a significant decrease in calorie intake but it is seen that when we go back to a normal diet we may probably gain weight again.

- In the same way, we often assume that low-fat or low-carb foods must be low-calorie healthy foods. But it is not the ultimate truth. Sometimes these healthy diet foods are loaded with harmful artificial sweeteners and preservatives but less in nutrients, therefore such food can create harmful effects on our health. Hence, we should check their ingredients before consuming them. In short, we should choose only nutrient-dense calorie deficit food for gaining healthy weight loss results.

- Crash diets are also very effective and give visual results but we must follow them under the supervision of an expert nutritionist because they can create several health issues like constipation, nausea, fatigue, hair fall, high levels of uric acid and even sometimes gall bladder stone formation. Therefore, we should be very conscious of following them.

- In recent years, a gluten-free diet is in trend for weight loss. People are opting for this diet even though they are not sensitive to gluten. Gluten is a protein found in wheat, barley and rye grains. Doctors recommend this diet to those who have celiac disease or are sensitive to gluten. But we should be aware that if we don't have these health problems, we must not avoid gluten as it contains many vitamins, fibre, and minerals. So, simply reducing gluten in the diet means that we have to find out other options to fulfil these requirements.
  Secondly, many gluten-free food products contain high calories, so before purchasing these products, we must check the calories they contain. Sometimes, when we opt for a gluten-free diet unnecessarily it can be a cause of double loss, as we are getting fewer nutrients but gaining more calories. Then we can imagine, how beneficial it can be for us.
  So, it doesn't matter what kind of diet we follow (vegetarian diet or non-vegetarian diet), we should just focus on their nutritious value and the calories they contain.

The main thing that matters: what we eat, how much we eat and how much physical activity we do determines whether we gain or lose weight. This is the sum-up code of weight loss. So, whenever we eat too much, our body stores excess calories as fat.

But simultaneously if we increase our exercise level according to calorie consumption, then we will not gain weight.

CHAPTER TEN

Can certain foods burn Fat?

Most of us perceive that some specific food can remove the toxins or burn fat from the body and they consume them in enormous amounts without knowing their limitations. As a result, they have to face some other health complications.

We should not forget that our body detoxifies itself naturally, some specific organs do the detox work. The spleen, liver, and kidney provide cleaning functions. But yes, we can give strength to them with the help of a nutritious and healthy diet, so that they can do their jobs efficiently. No food burns fat alone as it also depends on the type of food we have and how much water we intake. This food might produce short-term results but definitely, they don't produce long-term benefits. Let's know more about them:

Some foods having caffeine may speed up the metabolism for a short time but along with this, exercise is also essential for better results. No doubt, several juices (like amla, aloe vera, noni, lemon water, etc.) can help in the detoxification process and improve the digestion process but they can't do miracles on their own. Some norms have to be followed for visual results like drinking enough water, doing intense exercise, etc.

Protein shakes are considered the ideal tool for weight loss. However, protein indeed shakes help to make us feel full in the long run and reduce our appetite, but drinking too much of it is not safe for everyone, as it may not be suitable for people with pre-existing kidney problems that require protein restrictions. But only protein shakes cannot fulfil all the requirements of nutrients that the body needs. Therefore, it is important to plan the entire food intake under the supervision of fitness experts so that we can healthily lose weight.

Certain seeds like chia seeds, flax seeds, haleem seeds, etc. are very effective in weight loss too. But again, everyone can't take them because it is often seen that, just knowing their benefits, most people consume them on their own, but they might not be aware that it can be quite harmful to them if they are having high acidity problems or allergens.

Even if you are taking a blood-thinning medicine, you should consult your doctor first because these seeds can interfere with your medicine and create more health problems. So before consuming any of the seeds regularly, you should be more conscious about them.

Like that, we often think that herbs contain natural chemicals, so they can't be harmful to us and we can consume herbal weight loss products blindly. But the fact is, all herbal products are not safe to consume, because all herbs are not suitable for everyone, some people are allergic to specific herbs, and several herbs like Ginkgo Biloba, Ginger, etc. can create contradictions if they are not according to bodily doshas (Vata, pitta, Kapha). Few herbal products can cause diarrhoea, nausea, headache, and other health complications. Thus, for the safe side, we should consume only certified products and recommendations of qualified health practitioners.

That is why, it would be better, if we contemplate all these elements, to diagnose what is responsible for our weight gain before opting for a weight loss strategy. These weight loss misconceptions are so common that we don't even realize how they affect our health and can make the weight loss journey much harder, but we can make it better with our accurate knowledge and conscious efforts. This will transform our obesity into a fit and healthy body.

CHAPTER ELEVEN

Misconceptions about Exercising

While the mantra of "no pain, no gain" motivates to all for exercising, it can be dangerous when taken to the extreme. However, the level of exercise determines our fitness goals but when we overexert ourselves (to burn fat quickly) could undo the results. Even it can lower our fitness level. Along with, our negligible mistakes and wrong interpretations about exercise can put negative effects on our performance and health.

Let's know about these misconceptions and their facts so that we can develop the right schedule of exercise and appropriately achieve fitness goals.

Exercising all day and not getting appropriate results is now seen in the routine of every other person. We try various diet plans and exercise routines but nothing goes as we planned. It feels like nothing we do can change our shape which is false.

If we keep relying on the hit and trial method, it might take decades actually to find the right exercise routine for you. But if we acquire a bit of knowledge about our path and the misconceptions about it, then this might save time and make things easier. Knowing can change your overall perception of the meaning of exercise for you.

Most people think that by doing exercise regularly they can convert fat into muscles but actually, it is an erroneous thought. The fact is, exercise can't turn fat into muscle because fat and muscle are two different tissue types and one cannot be converted to the other. As muscle is an active tissue that burns calories and they are built when they break down and fill up with protein, whereas fat is simply a storage of excess energy in the body.

Here one thing should also be considered if we are doing intense exercises and still find that we are not losing weight, it may be that we are building muscle mass and these muscle tissues weigh more than fat. As a result, our body weight will remain the same although we lose fat content. In short, while doing moderate exercise daily we burn fat but gain muscle mass resulting in no change in weight.

A common misconception is that if we sweat more, we can burn more calories. But it is wrong because when we work hard, our body tends to heat up and releases heat through sweating as the purpose of sweating is to help regulate the body temperature. The amount we sweat is highly individual-oriented which is affected by certain factors such as air temperature, humidity, the clothes we wear, the body's tendency and our fitness level, etc. So the quantity of sweating can't be considered as the parameter, to measure how many calories we have burnt.

We know that if exercise is done in the right way, at the right time gives us the right benefits. It is believed that if we do intensive exercise for longer hours, the results will be better and quite faster, But the fact is that when we work out for longer hours, we feel stress in the body as our body starts secreting cortisol, which is a stress hormone. We feel a craving for eating something exciting, in this state, if we eat empty-calorie foods (foods that contain high calories but have fewer nutrients) can also be a cause of weight gain.

Likewise, most people perceive that exercise is a tiring task and if they do exercise, they can't do their routine work efficiently, but the fact may be quite different because, when we do exercise in a relaxed mood, it makes us feel more energetic. All health practitioners always encourage exercise because they believe exercise releases the endorphin hormone in the blood which is known as the happy hormone. So if we do exercise in a relaxing way it can be like a tonic for our health.

More often, it is seen that asthmatic and heart patients usually avoid doing exercise as they think it can create an adverse impact on their health. But we should not forget that exercise helps to strengthen the heart and lung muscles and improve the blood flow around the body. Also, it is an effective way for sending more oxygen to different organs and muscles. More of that it enhances the flexibility of muscles. Thus no doubt, light exercises can be beneficial for improving the health of those patients. They can do several light exercises in the sitting position or do simple but effective asanas in the presence of a yoga instructor. However, the type of exercise and the intensity will vary, depending upon the person's age, health, and fitness goals.

We also see that thin people avoid exercise as they think that they are already slim so they don't need to do exercise but they must be aware that as they have the least amount of muscles, their body weight might be lesser (as the muscle area is very dense). While exercising, these connective muscle tissues can tear and build up with proper nutrition, in this way, thin people get their bodies in shape. Thus, through exercise, they can build up their muscles and improve their body structure.

Therefore, we can say that exercise is beneficial not only for the obese but for everyone. But along with, we should also remain aware that for gaining maximum health benefits, the aim is to work hard but not too hard. As, when we do moderate or excess workouts daily, our body gets exhausted and can create numerous negative impacts on health such as fatigue, dizziness, headache, cramps, heart palpitation, etc. Sometimes it can damage the muscle, cartilage, ligaments, and joints also. Therefore, our body needs time (1-2 days once a week) to repair ourselves. For this, we should take proper rest for recovery. Also, we should intake calcium and antioxidants in appropriate amounts so that we can recover fast. For this, we can consume moringa, wheat grass, spirulina, etc. herbs with the guidance of health experts.

Most people consume whey protein when they do intense exercises for bodybuilding but here they must remain aware that whey protein should not be consumed on their own. The fitness trainers also say that it is not beneficial for all as it can create a lot of problems. For example, people suffering from kidney problems should not intake whey protein, as it contains nitrogen waste and needs a lot of water for filtering it by the kidney but if the kidney does not work properly then it tends to create some health issues. Similarly, if they are suffering from an Acne problem then whey protein can enhance this problem. Therefore whey protein should be consumed under the guidance of fitness experts only.

Like that, we often assume that we should always focus on burning the maximum calories through exercising to get the desired weight, but here we should not forget that pushing ourselves too hard can backfire and create frustration. Even regular intense exercises could have created some serious side effects like:

- When females workout too hard, they may miss their periods, then they should talk to their doctor. It may cause a reduction of estrogen levels in the body which can further lead to osteoporosis.

- Similarly, if you notice that the colour of urine has changed after moderate exercises, you must consult your doctor as it might be a signal that substances from damaged muscle tissue have leaked into the bloodstream. Even sometimes endurance exercise can create too much pressure on the heart to pump blood faster and over time it may lead to heart problems.

- Health practitioners noted that consistent exercise causes the body to produce endorphins (the hormone) to block pain and create feelings of happiness. Therefore if you find out that someone is working out consistently even in illness, they may be addicted to exercise. This psychological addiction further can create pretty serious problems.

Looking at the above discussion we can say that although exercise has numerous benefits, excess exercise can be worse for health, thereby it is important to understand its drawbacks so that we can remain injury-free and energetic.

These minor mistakes can become a barrier to achieving desirable results of weight loss. That is why it is important to understand its pitfalls to appropriately lead a healthier and fit life.

CHAPTER TWELVE

Interesting facts about Weight loss and Exercise

- A fat cell lives for about 7 years, when a fat cell dies a new one grows to replace it. The body keeps track of how many fat cells it has.

- Fat cells exist in all parts of the body except in the eyelids.

- Each fat cell can expand up to 10 times its normal size.

- A person can't reduce their total number of fat cells. New fat cells emerge during childhood and typically stop by adolescence. As an adult the number of fat cells remains the same, they just change their volumes as we gain or lose weight.

- The temperature in a person's bedroom may help boost weight loss efforts. It is quite interesting that colder sleepers burn more calories likely because their bodies were working harder to maintain a stable body temperature of 98.6*F

- Doctors determine that sleep deprivation can make it harder to lose weight because inadequate sleep upsets a person's hormone balance which decreases 'Leptin' (a hormone that makes a person feel full) and increases Ghrelin' (a hormone that triggers hunger). That might be the reason when we wake up late at night, we crave something to eat. So, it might be a bit amusing that sleep is the cheapest and easiest obesity medicine.

- We always think that most fat exits from our body through bodily fluids like sweat, urine, tears, etc. but actually, we lose enough fat in the form of carbon dioxide that leaves our body through the lungs.

- Body fat distribution changes with age. For example, pre-menopausal women have a higher level of subcutaneous belly fat while menopausal women tend to have a higher level of visceral fat. (this is likely due to a decreasing level of estrogen hormone)

- Fat is not our enemy. Our body will function optimally only when it has an appropriate amount of fat deposition because fat is living tissue and capable of producing several essential hormones that control metabolism, it is helpful in neurological functions. That is why people with ultra-low fat suffer a lot of health problems.

- It is believed that muscle needs more calories to maintain itself than any other body tissue. Therefore, if we have more muscles, we can burn more calories.

- The body starts to burn muscle instead of fat after just 20 minutes of intense cardio exercise such as: walking on a treadmill, running, spinning, etc. That is why fitness instructors advise us to take a break between workouts and then restart so that we reduce fat only.

- We generally perceive that calories are associated with food and drink only but the fact is, anything that contains energy has calories. For example, 1 kilogram of coal contains 7,000,000 calories.

- Keep yourself busy if you want to lose weight. You often notice that when we indulge ourselves in creative activities, we often forget about having meals. It means our body doesn't require as much food as we pamper ourselves with it. We need to be aware that some weight loss Diet plans might create gallstones. The reason is, that when we follow a low-calorie diet and lose weight too quickly, the liver starts to secrete extra cholesterol. This can lead to enough cholesterol in the bile also causing gallstones. That is why we should always follow these diet plans under the supervision of health experts so that we can healthily get desirable results.

- It is believed that the person who is sitting for a long time (about 8-9 hours), the secretion of fat-burning enzymes is decreased in their bodies and they easily gain weight.

- If we are trying to lose fat, the three most considerable sections of the food label are Serving size, Servings per container, and Calories per serving. So, before purchasing them, we should read them carefully, because if there are two servings and we eat both. Unfortunately, we gain double the calories, double the fat and can cause double the trouble.

- In the tapeworm diet, some people swallow tapeworms to help them lose weight. But we need to know that the tapeworm might lay eggs in other tissues such as the nervous system, which can cause serious health complications.

- There is no Perfect Diet for everyone as all people are unique. Subtle differences in genetics, body type, physical activity and environment can affect which type of diet we should follow. The fact is, what works for one person may not be perfect for the other.

Hope these have enlightened your mind to new facts but the knowledge is endless. It always feels less when you crave to know more.

Yoga

The practice of Yoga is ancient and also mysterious. There are many concepts regarding Yoga that is not very clear to most people. So if we start to follow yoga norms, first we should understand its inherent principles and concepts, so that we can opt for it without any confusion.

CHAPTER THIRTEEN

Misconceptions about Asanas

Asana is a way to do conscious breathing that improves flexibility, strength, and balance in the body and also evokes a relaxation response. Asana is not as simple as it is often considered and should not be done forcefully. It requires proper warming up before starting. Even incorrect postures can harm the internal organs and can create some health issues.

If you feel any discomfort in a pose and upon release, it feels better, it is probably the stretch of connective tissue or muscle that you are feeling, which is fine.

But if you experience pain even when you come out of the posture, it may be joint tenders or ligaments giving you an indication that you need to examine the related area. That is why it is always advised that you should do asanas under the guidance of qualified yoga teachers so that you can do asanas in the right way without any harm.

The second thing which must be considered is that asanas should not be performed continuously because asanas are not physical exercise. Rather it is a technique to put pressure on a particular gland and stimulate hormone secretions in the body. That is why it is necessary to keep a short gap between the two asanas and take a rest for a moment to normalize the hormonal secretion from that gland.

Another most common mistake is that most people prefer to do asanas in groups, but it can be harmful to them because everyone has different health issues and different body types. Then how can we do asanas in a large group without knowing their pre-health problems?

But yes, a group of people with the same health problems can do simple asanas together but nothing more than that. Anyhow if you do asanas in a group it is better to inform about your health issues to the yoga instructor so that the trainer can guide you on which particular asana you should not perform.

Many people just avoid doing asanas as they assume that asanas are only for flexible people but it is erroneous thought, the fact is, flexibility is certainly not a requirement to start practising asana, as we all are not super flexible but we will improve gradually when we do it regularly. Tentatively, we will see a drastic improvement in our strength and flexibility. There are so many simple asanas that will help to convert the stiff body to become more flexible. So undoubtedly we should do them regularly.

But yes we will always remain conscious that everyone has their stamina and they perform according to that. So, we should not force ourselves to do difficult asanas just because we think they would be beneficial for our health, as if we are not comfortable then it might harm our body tissues and organs. That is why it is always encouraged that asana must be done according to the individual's flexibility with care and in the comfort zone.

This means the asanas will be beneficial to health only when it is practised in a particular way. In short, we can say that it needs our enthusiasm, discipline, and consistency for giving fruitful results.

CHAPTER FOURTEEN

Misconceptions about Meditation

Ancient sagas define meditation as an art of bringing harmony to body, mind, and consciousness. It is the way to meet our soul and reach ultimate power. But somehow there is a lot of confusion we have, regarding meditation which should be clarified, to gain optimum benefits of it.

In general, we assume that meditation means concentrating the mind at one point, but one logical thought is that meditation is not concentration because in concentration we put efforts to control the mind and we know that when we focus on something forcefully we lose energy. Somehow this is the reason that some people when they have finished the meditation, feel tired because they are fighting and fighting to limit their thoughts. It is impossible to become completely thoughtless. Thereby when people try to think of nothing they often think more because thinking is as natural to the mind as hearing is to our ears.

On the other hand, meditation is a way to give relaxation to the mind, it should be effortless and peaceful when you forget the outer world and your body and just attach to your soul. Means to say, the aim of meditation is not to stop thinking. It is to be more aware of thinking so that our thoughts don't control us and when you meditate as such, you will feel more energized. The ideology is, that when we struggle less with our body, we experience more natural peace.

Secondly, meditation doesn't necessarily involve sitting in silence or any particular position. You can sit comfortably on a chair or a sofa, it is all fine. Just focus that your spine remains straight and clothes are not tight when you do meditation. All you have to do is, relax your neck, shoulder, and head and in this state try to allow the body to connect with your inner self. Here the idea is to focus your full attention on your breath. With routine practice, you begin to be internally aware that you should not give and take negative thoughts. This is the prime and the most important form of meditation. Gradually, you can see the world more objectively and can do meditation internally. Then, it will not matter to you how many people are around you.

Besides this, it is believed that meditation is just a way to relieve stress, anxiety, or depression but meditation is much more than just stress reduction. It gets you in direct contact with life and your daily experiences. When you start to follow the rules of meditation properly, you will find a drastic change in your personality as sattva guna increases and you will become a more joyful and lovable person and your way of thinking become more positive. Thus, the impacts of meditation are enormous, we can't bind it only for specific disorders.

Even many people have this wrong interpretation about meditation that if they do meditation daily, they will lose their edge, because they believe that as meditation can increase sattva guna in them, then they will become softer and won't be able to handle tough situations. But it is not true, you will ever notice that when you get internally calm, you can face difficult situations more efficiently. Even Meditation sharpens your focus and heightens your performance because it works on your thought process and of course, makes you mentally strong.

In such a way, meditation is a powerful tool for anyone. So, what kind of spiritual views you have, what lifestyle you lead etc. it all doesn't matter. Meditation is a way to detox negative thinking, improve your mental strength and enhance your personality. Anyhow if you cannot spare much time for meditation then you can start meditation with 5 minutes a day, slowly you will realize that you will have more control over your thoughts and you will feel more energized and rejuvenated.

Meditation offers a myriad of health benefits. It depends on us how much we can gain. Thus, we can say that yoga is a path to healthy living, we should opt for it as soon as we can. Like anything else in life, improvement comes with practice, so when we practise yoga regularly we feel drastic improvement in our physical and mental health.

CHAPTER FIFTEEN

Misconceptions about Yoga

We perceive that yoga is a way to calm the mind and body but it is the wrong perception because yoga cannot be done correctly in a stressed state, on the contrary yoga must be done with a calm and still mind to get the best results.

When the mind is relaxed, breath is drawn from the left nostril and the "Ida Nadi" is active. The Ida Nadi correlates to the right hemisphere of the brain and the body is in rest mode. Ida Nadi signals a state of calm serenity. In this state, we should do yoga for gaining optimum benefits.

But when we are stressed, Nadis (nerves) would be blocked and the 'Parana' flow is constructed. In this state, mostly the right nostril (the Pingala Nadi) is active which increases the acid level in the body and heals the body. At this time if we do energetic exercise then they are more beneficial for us like we can eat a meal which is digested easily or we can take part in sports games or do intense exercises, but we should not do meditation or yoga.

Most people think Yoga means asanas but actually, Yoga is a very vast concept. It is the union of the body, mind, and soul. It is concerned about our diet, daily routine, habits, lifestyle, and way of thinking. Although yoga practise starts with the body, the ultimate goal should be to go deeper within and find our true selves.

On the whole, Yoga is not as simple as it seems. It is not a single practice. It has eight unique branches called 'Ashtanga Yoga' for the development of one's true personality. They are:

- **Yama**: The Code of ethics.
- **Niyama**: Disciplines for daily routine
- **Asanas**: Yoga pastures
- **Pranayama**: Breath discipline
- **Pratyahara**: healthy diet
- **Dharana**: Inner focus on the higher chakras
- **Dhyana**: Meditation
- **Samadhi**: Dissolution of self in the highest realm

Through these yoga codes, we can improve our physical, mental, and spiritual health but it is not as simple as that, it is a systematic process. There should be a perfect understanding of what to do and what not to do, also with the adverse effects of certain procedures.

Practising yoga, asanas or kriyas is not suitable for all. As, if it is done in the wrong way, it can be drastic for health. That is why, the people who learn yoga through books and practice it on their own, can create serious complications regarding health. Therefore, for the safe side, before starting yoga, we should understand the limitations of our body first and then practice yogic exercises accordingly.

Some rules regarding meals must be followed such as; when, how much, and what kind of meal we can have before and after the yoga. Therefore it is said that you should always practice yoga under the supervision of experienced teachers. Means to say, yoga seems very simple but actually, it is very complicated. That is why it has to be done with perfect understanding and proper guidance.

Many people hesitate to start yoga just because they think that, as they have some health issues so they can't do yoga properly. But the fact is, yoga can be started at any age and under any health condition. It just requires dedication and regular practice. Asthmatics and heart patients can do pranayama, as breathing exercises give the required oxygen to the lungs in sufficient quantity which will help to reduce the effect of various diseases to a great extent. Asanas also boost muscular strength and improve the blood flow in the body. Moreover, through meditation, we can also ease many health concerns like stress, anxiety, depression, etc. Even if we start doing Yoga in childhood it impacts our physical and mental health very deeply and can change our personality in a very positive way.

If it is not possible to give much time to yoga, we can start it up with 15 minutes as:

- 6 minutes of warm-up exercises
- 6 minutes Surya asanas
- 3 minutes pranayama

It is also not necessary that we should do yoga in the morning only, rather yoga can be done at any time of the day only your stomach should be quite empty (3 hours after any meal). In this manner, yoga will not create obstacles to the daily routine. Even we can get tremendous benefits from yoga with minor changes in diet also. However, yoga does encourage a vegetarian diet as vegetarian food is often digested easily and provides almost all nutrients to the body but if necessary the non-vegetarian food can be consumed, it is truly an individual's choice.

This way, with regular practice of yoga, we feel more relaxed and fit and want to adopt other yoga codes, thus yoga is never forced to change the lifestyle completely, but we do it willingly.

Ayurveda

Ayurveda is 5000 years old science. It teaches us how to lead physically, mentally, and spiritually healthy life. It is one of the safest paths to remain healthy and fit because it doesn't focus only on disease, rather it believes in building the body's natural system strong so that our body can more easily defend against disease.

But unfortunately, Ayurveda is associated with a handful of myths and misconceptions because somehow we interpret Ayurveda notions in the wrong way. Therefore, it is necessary to clear them out, otherwise, Ayurveda practices with inadequate awareness may do only harm, rather than being beneficial.

CHAPTER SIXTEEN

Ayurveda is not only a Herbal Treatment

Ayurvedic treatment is not only a herb-based treatment but is a vast concept and a mix of multiple things. In many cases, Ayurveda treatment can be done just with changes in our routine diet or lifestyle. Several times the patient is cured through only yogic exercise, meditation and detoxification or different therapies.

It works on many aspects such as, what kind of diet should be taken along with Ayurveda medicine, actually half of the treatment is based on it. Sometimes some seeds and food are restricted because they are not suitable for a particular person's body tendency (Vata, Pitta, Kapha). Some therapies are often recommended for more effective results like acupressure therapy, mud therapy, hydrotherapy, massage therapy, guasa therapy etc. Therefore proper scientific study and diagnosis are needed for effective treatment.

Ayurveda believes that the body can heal on its own, therefore we should give strength to the body with the right nutrients and therapies. But, the time required to cure any ailment, depends on several factors like:

- How soon the problem was diagnosed.
- Its severity,
- Patients' response to controlling their diet.
- And taking precautions etc.

We can say that Ayurveda works from the root cause of the disease and tries to uproot them gradually.

CHAPTER SEVENTEEN

Can Ayurveda cure all diseases?

There is no doubt that Ayurveda has myriad health benefits and it can cure a lot of diseases if they are in the initial stage but not all. In ancient times, it might have been cured, as at that time the immunity of people was very strong and their lifestyle was very accurate and simple. Their diets were according to Ayurvedic rules. Even the food was organic, the environment was clean, no pollution, no radiation, and no impurities in water, and even people worked hard and did pranayama, yoga, meditation, etc. regularly.

But in modern times, because of our luxurious lifestyles, environmental pollution, radiation, toxins, unhealthy diet, etc., our immunity level is getting lower every day. Therefore, it might not be possible to cure all diseases. But yes, Ayurveda treatment can decrease the severity of disease and reduce the time duration of diseases.

As most Ayurvedic natural remedies do not interfere with body resistance and at the same time, they are safer from side effects. That is why in the modern age, its charm is on the swing, and most health-conscious people prefer to adopt Ayurveda treatment because of its tremendous results.

CHAPTER EIGHTEEN

Herbal treatment is not always safe

The most disastrous misconception about Ayurveda is that its treatment is always safe for everyone and anybody can adopt it anytime. Herbs are natural, doesn't mean they are safe as many of the herbs used in Ayurveda contain several harmful toxins and molecules. They are safe and medicinally effective only when taken in appropriate quantities and with the proper mixture of the right ingredients.

Even though many herbal plants are toxic, these herbs are an effective treatment for certain diseases and can give tremendous results but only when they are given by a trained herbalist, otherwise they can cause some serious health issues.

Another big mistake, which is mostly done by people, is that, as Ayurveda medicines are herbal and natural, many people choose to self-medicate themselves with overheard Ayurveda remedies. But they have no idea that if in any form, the quantity and combination of herbs are not correct, it can create dangerous consequences. Even sometimes, its side effects could be drastic and can create serious health issues. Inadequate herbal treatment can be dangerous when taken during pregnancy or in an advanced stage of some critical diseases. We also note that some seeds like chia seeds and flax seeds can interfere with blood-thinning medications. The well-known spice turmeric (curcumin) can elevate the deficiency of iron content in the anaemic. Therefore we can't consume all kinds of herbs as they have myriad health benefits. That is why it is always advised that all herbs should be taken under the guidance of health practitioners.

However, Ayurveda medicines are derived from herbs and they have foul taste and odour but it is essential to be bitter because they are required by the body to perform the cleansing act effectively. Anyhow, nowadays, it is not as difficult to take herbs as in earlier times because many Ayurveda pharmaceutical companies are making it easy to eat in the form of tablets and capsules (supplements).

As we see that Ayurveda has adverse effects too and if not taken properly can lead to dangerous results. But if ayurvedic treatment can be drastic too then why do we trust it so much. And the question arises if it is safe or not.

CHAPTER NINETEEN

Are Ayurveda medicines safe for consumption?

Ayurvedic medicines are made up of natural minerals & herbs and are safe to consume under some rules and regulations which we must be aware of them before opting for any ayurvedic treatment. Even if they are prepared by pharmaceutical companies, these manufacturers must follow some strict rules described by the food department association. Thus, strong chemicals should not be used in Ayurveda medicines.

More of that, some firm guidelines have been established for quality control and standard of Ayurveda medicines in the country such as:

- **PLIM** – Pharmacopoeial laboratory of Indian Medicine
- **CCRAS** – Central Council of Research in Ayurvedic Science has published the Protocol for Testing of Ayurvedic medicines. Moreover, several drug testing laboratories are established throughout the country to check the quality of Ayurveda medicine. Manufacturers of Ayurvedic Medicines must get certified by these laboratories regarding the quality and stability of their products. In this way, the consumer gets tested and genuine products.

For the safe side, the consumer must purchase these medicines from registered Ayurvedic Practitioners and reliable brands.

Can we take herbal medicines along with allopathic medicines?

As Ayurvedic herbs are potent, some herbs can interact with allopathic medications but not all. Tentatively, it is seen that many common herbs like ginger, ginkgo Biloba, ginseng etc. somehow can interfere with some specific allopathic medicines like anticoagulants and antipsychotic drugs etc. But a qualified herbal practitioner knows which herb can react adversely and guide us properly. Therefore, it is always important to check for contradiction before taking any new herbal treatment with allopathic medicines and vice versa.

But in general, many herbs are gentle and nutritive and an abundant source of vitamins and minerals, which the body needs to repair itself. So they can be used with other medications.

On the whole, Ayurvedic treatment is very comprehensive. Although its techniques are ancient but effective. So there is no doubt that Ayurveda can be a boon if we adopt its concepts in the right way.

Traditions and Health Benefits

India is a land of wise, intellectual, and devotional sages and monks. These sages interpret 'the Vedas and Upanishads very well. These Holy Scriptures have laid down various codes to bring spirituality into human awareness. Our ancestors have been practising them over the years which are considered now superstitions, but actually, these traditions are carried out for a specific purpose. However we follow them perpetually, but surprisingly we may not be even aware that a treasure of virtuous health is hidden in them.

Therefore, it might be beneficial for us if we know: What are they, and how can they influence our health? If we understand them logically then probably we could systematically follow them.

CHAPTER TWENTY

Colours can furnish Health benefits

Probably, it is quite surprising for many how colours can impact our health. But yoga and Ayurveda use different colours for the treatment of mental and physical ailments. How do they use these colours in therapies and what is the science behind them, if we understand it properly, then we might be astonished, by their majestic concepts.

We live in colours, as colours are all around us and every colour is unique because each colour has its vibration and also has a specific effect on the body.

It is a significantly known fact that there is an electromagnetic field around every object in this world. This electromagnetic field refers to an "Aura" composed of different layers of colours. Each colour is associated with a specific energy centre in the body called "Chakras". Chakra means a spinning wheel that creates a vacuum in the centre and draws in the energy from its surroundings which are considered Aura.

When ratios of colour in the body change, the body gets imbalanced. It gives rise to various ailments but when the colours are balanced, diseases are easily cured. To overcome the deficiency, to normalize excess colour, many colour therapies are used like sunlight, coloured textiles, gemstones, water processing colour therapy and different coloured artificial lights etc., in naturopathy this therapy is also known as chromo therapy.

It is believed that every cell is capable of emitting light and light is composed of colours. Each colour generates electrical impulses and fields of energy that can rejuvenate hormones and may start biochemical reactions in the body. It starts the healing process.

Light is considered to be one of the purest healing forces in the universe. The presence or absence of light can affect the hypothalamus, pituitary and pineal gland. This, in turn, can influence our physical and mental health.

CHAPTER TWENTY-ONE

Impact of colours in daily life

To know in detail the effect of colours on us, it's important that we first know how light works and colours are formed. The colours we see are determined by the wavelength of light that is reflected. We don't see colours with our eyes, we see colours with our brain.

Light enters the body through the eyes and skin. Our eyes have three types of cones: blue, green and red. The red cones are more sensitive to red wavelengths. Blue cones to blue wavelengths and Green cones to green wavelengths.

When a colour is reflected from an object, the light wavelength hits the eyes and light-sensitive cells (known as cones in the retina) send electrochemical signals to the visual cortex of the brain for processing, after that some retinal ganglion cells respond to light by sending signals mainly to a central brain region (called the hypothalamus). Then, the hypothalamus sends signals to the pineal gland and from there to the pituitary gland, (which regulates hormones in the body). When the brain starts processing this information, it results in hormonal changes in the body. Thus, our brain associates the wavelength with a colour.

These wavelengths impact our organs, blood, body system and everything else that composes the body. We can understand the frequency and impact of the colour wavelength from the chart below:

Colour	Range of Wavelength in nanometer (nm)	Psychological Implementation
Red	644	Passionate, aggressive, strength, sexuality, alertness, confidence, power
Orange	510	Happiness, Youthfulness, Friendly, devotional
Yellow	590	Mental stability, Concentration, Warning, activate the centre of brain.
Green	538	Natural, stable, optimistic, Prosperous
Blue	453.5	Serene, trustworthy, inviting, feeling of Safety
Indigo	445	Luxurious, Mysterious
Violet	400	Calmness, soothing
Black		Neutral, formal, gloomy, powerful, mysterious
White		Clean, pure, healthy

Colour Wavelength Chart

Thus, light with its component colours has a prominent impact on us so it can be used for healing the mind, body and spirit. This is the basic principle behind colour therapy. Unknowingly, we experience it in daily life:

- Exposure to light in the morning prompts. The release of the hormone 'cortisol' stimulates and wakes us and inhibits the release of melatonin. In the late evening, as the amount of blue light in sunlight is reduced, melatonin is released into the bloodstream and we become drowsy.

- There are some concerns about the excessive use of smartphones and tablets in the late evening, which can affect sleep quality because they emit a substantial amount of blue/ green light at a wavelength that inhibits the release of melatonin.

- Interestingly, people tend to gamble and take risks more, under red lights. It is no wonder that this is the predominant reason for the red colour choice in Casino atmospheres.

- Even our veins look blue because subcutaneous fat only allows blue light to penetrate the skin. Secondly, most veins carry deoxygenated blood which is darker in colour than oxygenated blood.

Colours deeply impact our minds and body. In colour therapy, we can use different colours to balance and maintain health in numerous ways like we can paint our house or room in specific colours, decorate our home with flowers, change the colour of curtains, light a candle of a certain colour, intake water from colour water bottles which are processed in sunrays, use light therapy or even simply wear coloured sunglasses.

Somehow we will also notice the correlation between the colour of food as red and orange colour foods look more tempting than other ones. We often experience that our brain will recognize a shade of colour to an assigned task faster than text alone.

CHAPTER TWENTY-TWO

Different colours, different Emotions

Mysteriously different colours provoke different emotions which is why they are used as symbols to convey different messages to the people, such as:

- Most of the baby products are white to symbolize – innocence and purity.
- Doctors and nurses wear white to emphasize - cleanliness.
- In the courtroom, advocates wear black and white which indicate- lie and truth.
- Indian brides mostly wear Red because the red colour is merely visible and makes a person confident, energetic and lovable.
- Green colour indicates neutral and natural, that is why most organic food brands choose a green colour to show their product's genuineness.
- The banking sector mostly chooses Blue colour in its Logo for showing its trustworthiness.
- Priests wear white colour to indicate that our soul is pure.

Why do Sadhus wear Orange Colour clothes?

In a spiritual realm, saffron is a symbol of sun and fire which provides us energy. As fire can burn all impurities and turn down to ashes, the sadhus might be trying to transmit the message that they have moved beyond the material realm and burnt all their luxurious desires. Also, fire facilitates a connection to purity and provides us with piousness. When sadhus wear saffron colour, they might be trying to convey that they have imbibed these values into their lives.

CHAPTER TWENTY-THREE

Gemstones and their colours

As light reflects, it refracts too. As light reflects and affects us, think about how a refracted light might impact us. Some stones are said to refract light, which in turn can be used to improve our lifestyle in many ways too.

Light is refracted into different stones to produce energy. Various gemstones are better than others in refraction. Very often we all wear different types of gemstones to strengthen our emotions and also empower our bodies. But most of us don't know what the gemstones are, how they work in our body, why we need to wear them etc. So, it is important to be aware of it.

The majority of gemstones are minerals. Natural gemstones are simply chemical compositions, in the shape of crystal structures formed in rocks. These are identified through their hardness and optical properties. Every gemstone has its unique chemical and atomic structure. Interestingly, many minerals are colourless in their pure form and it is the inclusion of impurities in their structure which leads to their colouration.

- Red Ruby - chromium + corundum
- Green Emerald - chromium + beryl
- Diamonds are made of carbon,
- Sapphires of aluminium chloride and so on.

As different colours of light have different wavelengths when a gemstone absorbs a certain wavelength of light, it can cause a transfer of electrons between ions, which affects colours. Because each wavelength carries a specific amount of energy. The result is that gemstones vary in colour.

In such a way, stones absorb these cosmic energies from the celestial bodies, in the form of colour-coded frequencies, through our solar system, which are then infused into our bodies through pendants or rings. For this reason, gems are worn on specific points of the body and make sure that they can touch the body point properly so that they can provide the relevant help to the body.

Along with that, these gemstones are suggested to be worn on a particular finger because according to acupressure therapy, below the fingers and on the fingers there are marmas (acupressure points) that are linked with different organs of the body. When the wearer puts pressure on these points, this has an impact on the health of the person either good or bad. Many times, it is seen that after wearing a gemstone some people get sick because putting the unrequired pressure over the marma can also harm their health. That is why it is said that gemstones should always be worn carefully.

CHAPTER TWENTY-FOUR

Importance of Havana

Havana is an ancient tradition. It is believed that Havana is a way to purify the atmosphere and the environment. When the samagri (many herbs and some food items) burn in the fire, it lets out smoke and fragrance, which helps to purify the environment.

- **Air**: when the huge Havana is performed, the air touches the fire, gets purified, and becomes lighter. This light air goes up and replaces the cold air. In such a way this process continues and air keeps getting purified till Havana is being performed.

- **Mango woods**: Moreover, the fire is fueled with different kinds of wood and herbs. The smoke produced by the fire purifies the air by killing harmful bacteria as the main ingredient used in Havana is mango wood. When burnt, it releases Formic Aldehyde (a type of gas) which is used for killing harmful bacteria.

- **Guggal**: Guggal also is an antibiotic herb that helps to kill harmful bacteria and cleanse the air.

- **Ghee**: Cow Ghee is a very important and essential ingredient, and is used in Havana. When ghee is burnt, the fat particles get laden on the dust particles in the atmosphere which again come back to the earth in the form of rain, thus helping to nourish the vegetation.

- **Aromatic herbs**: Dalchini, Lavang, rose petals, cardamom, amla, Kapoor, nutmeg, coconut, etc. When these aromatic herbs are burnt together, they remove the foul odour in the atmosphere through their fragrance and Havana's smoke has the potency to kill fungi and harmful bacteria. Thus, performing Havana regularly can protect us from a lot of diseases.

During Havana chanting mantras fills our body with positive energies. These powerful mantras activate a particular kind of energy in the different parts of the body, gradually stress starts to disappear and increases the feeling of relaxation and we feel internally more calm and energetic.

At present times, when a polluted environment has become the biggest challenge for the entire living world. Frequent performing Havana can give a relevant contribution to purifying the environment. It will also help in the removal of various diseases causing viruses and harmful bacteria. The sound waves created by chanting during Havana purify the mind. Means to say, the purpose of Havana is to enhance the energy of the human body and make it healthy and progressive. In this manner, the doer of Havana greatly serves the entire universe.

CHAPTER TWENTY-FIVE

Logic behind chanting Mantras

We often recite mantras, but don't know what the logic to chant them is and how can impact our health and life. These mantras seem very simple but when we analyze this concept, it surprises us with their uniqueness.

As every molecule of our body emits energy, our thoughts, mind, body, and spirit emit energy in the form of vibrations. According to Veda-Puranas, chanting is that mystic vibration that activates all the senses and raises a level of self-awareness. These rhythmic pronunciations and vibrations have a calming effect on the body and the nervous system which gradually fills our body with positive energy.

The chanting sound has its importance. If you want to gain optimum benefits from chanting mantras then you have to pronounce them in a very correct rhythm, because when you utter a sound, a form is being created. There is a whole science of using sounds in a particular way so that it creates the right kind of emotions.

The basic concept of sound

Sound is made up of vibrations, these vibrations are produced from a source, travel through the air, and then are picked up by the ear, before being interpreted by the brain, which assigns them some value. The number of vibrations per second is known as frequency because all matter is a component of atomic material, which is in constant motion, thus, everything and everyone vibrates at some frequency.

Chant OM

Om is not just a sound, it's a wave of the universe. Everything around us is pulsating and vibrating as if nothing is standing still. The word OM is defined by ancient scripture, as being the primordial sound of creation. It is the original vibration of the universe. From this first vibration, all other vibrations can manifest.

The sound OM when chanted, vibrates at the frequency of 432 H2, which is the same vibrational frequency found throughout everything in nature. As OM is the basic sound of the universe, by chanting it, we are symbolically and physically acknowledging our connection to nature.

Reciting the OM mantra purifies the environment around us and creates positive energy that makes us feel happier and stress-free. Also, chanting OM helps our mind and body to energize. Furthermore, it helps us to improve our immunity system, generate self-healing power and even save us from many diseases.

Chanting Om can give us relief from sinus problems as when we chant Om a vibration sound is felt through our vocal cord that clears and opens up the sinuses. Chanting Om also has cardiovascular benefits as it reduces stress and relaxes the body, which tends to bring down the blood pressure to the normal level.

The rhythmic pronunciation of Om also calms down the amygdala of the brain (anger centre of the brain) and decreases stress. Thus, those who do the meditation of OM daily will get tremendous health benefits.

Chanting Gayatri Mantra

Gayatri Mantra is a very powerful mantra. It produces almost 110,000 different kinds of waves per second. It is strongly believed that chanting Gayatri Mantra helps to calm the mind and release relaxing hormones. It also helps stimulate the chakras and give therapeutic effects to the body.

Chant mantras 108 times

It is believed that certain brain parts are activated when we recite mantras. It is a very powerful and positive vibration that clears all negativity from our minds so chanting a mantra can decrease stress, anxiety, and even depressive symptoms. It also boosts feelings of relaxation and mental calmness.

According to Ayurveda, –we have 108 marma pol (vital points of life forces) in our body. Positive and correct chanting can enhance the strength of these vital points as our thoughts, actions, and words create vibrations of unique frequencies, it fills our body with a lot of positivity and calmness.

Secondly, 108 can be noticed with a relationship with the sun, earth, and moon. The diameter of the sun multiplied 108 times gives us the distance from the earth to the sun and correspondingly the diameter of the moon multiplied 108 times, gives us the distance from the earth to the moon.

Somehow 108 becomes an amazing cosmic ratio of the closest two plants that affect the earth and human fortunes. It is amazing.

CHAPTER TWENTY-SIX

Interesting facts about Chakras

In Ayurveda and natural science, it is believed that our body is not only a physical and mental structure, it is also an energetic system, called chakras.

Do chakras exist or not?

Chakras do not appear as organs and tissues in the body, their presence cannot be proven. That is why most people might be denying being there. But natural science and Ayurveda define their authenticity very well.

The ancient sages believed that our chakras govern bodily systems, perhaps they are metaphors for energy. But because the chakras are invisible, therefore its existence is questionable. We accept that matter and energy are integrally related, yet the Body is matter and visible. Chakras are energy and are invisible.

These energy centres impact both body and mind functions. But where they are and how they influence our body and mind are debatable. However, several postulated theories are available in Vedic scriptures. Somehow every experienced doctor believes that the mind influences the body, though there is no proven evidence, even cell signalling communication systems are widely accepted.

Similarly, chakras represent the various energy points in our body, which are subtle but when controlled properly, can produce effective results, but they cannot be measured because they are more to do with emotions and feelings rather than with physical touch.

The body is electrical and the nervous system and brain are largely electrochemical machines. Water is an excellent electrical conductor. An even better conductor of electricity than water is blood. Each heartbeat creates an electrical pulse throughout the entire circulatory system which we can feel and measure.

The interaction of electricity and magnetism creates an electromagnetic field in and around the body. Thus, as human beings, we radiate a very low level of electricity that's known as an electromagnetic field. Every organ and even every cell has its electromagnetic field. Thus, collectively they form a measurable electromagnetic field.

Similarly, "prana" is the subtle life energy in the form of air and breath which flows in every part of the body, yet it is invisible. But, when this prana Vayu imbalances, we can experience physical issues like hypertension, restlessness and shortness of breath etc. So, if something is invisible it doesn't mean that they don't exist. Just like air, chakras also are not visible but they exist in the realm of our mind which is evoked through our own emotions, we experience immense power for healing our ailments.

The Location of the chakras

It is believed that all seven chakras are located on the spine and the spinal cord is the pathway for messages sent by the brain to the body and from the body to the brain.

There are three main nadis in the body, the Ida, Pingala and Sushumna. They all start at the base of the spine and travel upwards to the head. The Ida and Pingala Nadi go upwards and connect to opposite nostrils as Ida Nadi connect to the left nostril and Pingala Nadi connect to the right nostril, while the Sushumna Nadi travels straight up to the crown of the head. It is believed that where the Ida and Pingala cross each other and intersect with the Sushumna that place is the chakra's place.

Prana is considered the bioelectrical energy that flows throughout our body, especially along the spine. If the quality and amount of prana are optimum, then chakra is energized and the enzymes and hormones secrete properly, the efficiency of vital organs is improved, as result, we gain better health.

It is believed that each chakra rotates at a specific frequency. They are associated with the organs and glands of the particular region, where they are located, and radiate a specific colour and energy. Such as:

- **Root Chakra** (Mooladhara) It influences:- the reproduction system It is located at the base of the spine between the anus and the genitals.

- **Sacral Chakra** (Swadhisthana) influences:- the adrenal gland. It is located in the lower abdomen about four fingers below the navel.

- **Solar Plexus Chakra** (Manipura) influences:- Pancreas It is located at the solar plexus, between the navel and the bottom of the rib cage.

- **Heart Chakra** (Anahata) it influences:-Thymus gland is located in the heart region.

- **Throat Chakra** (Vishuddha) influences the Thyroid gland - located at the base of the throat coinciding with the thyroid gland.

- **Third Eye Chakra** (Aagya) influences:- Pituitary gland Which is located between the eyebrows. It is often used as a focal point during asana practice to develop more concentration and awareness.

- **Crown Chakra** (Sahastrara) influences:- Pineal gland It is located on the crown of the head.

It is the centre of spirituality, energy, enlightenment and dynamic thoughts. It allows for the inward flow of wisdom and brings the gift of cosmic consciousness. Thus, each chakra is related to the particular body system. Since they are interrelated, when one of them is imbalanced, it causes a disturbance in the functionality of the other chakras as well.

Ancient yogis insist on doing pranayama, chanting mantras and meditation so that our chakras get energized and we remain healthy.

CHAPTER TWENTY-SEVEN

Why people wear Rudraksha?

Although found common in India in many places, rudraksha is yet being ignored for its benefits. Rudraksha has come up in many Hindu scriptures so there might be a reason that this small seed was so popular in these texts.

Rudraksha, the seed is from a large evergreen tree of the genus Elaeocarpus. It is believed that Rudraksha has electromagnetic properties that work magically on our bodies. It heals many ailments and also increases the positive flow of energy in the body.

The rudraksha beads range from "one faced to 21 faced" and each of them has different traits. They emit different frequencies as per their mukhis. When worn on the body, these frequencies resonate with corresponding body chakras and give a calming impression on our mind and body.

Rudraksha is worn near the heart so that it exerts a right force around the heart which improves its performance, controls the heartbeat, and maintains the blood circulation.

The yogis believe that Rudraksha beads have anti-inflammatory and anti-bacterial properties. So drinking the water of soaked Rudraksha will build the resistance to various diseases. In this manner, the Rudraksha beads act as a protective shield for the body.

Why do Sages wear Rudraksha?

Most of the Sages wear Rudraksha for meditation purposes and also to maintain the blood circulation in the body because they meditate usually in hilly areas.

The second reason is – As Sadhus and Sanyasis were continuously on the move, they could not drink water from any pond because the water might have been poisoned or contaminated in the forest. They use Rudraksha beads to identify whether the food and water that they are about to consume are pure or not. They pour water over a Rudraksha, if it moves at the clockwise discretion then it is safe for consumption. If it moves anticlockwise, the water is not supposed to be consumed. The same process they are following to check the food (cooked) also.

But we get rudraksha's benefits only then when it is original. Therefore before purchasing the rudraksha, we should first check its originality, which can be tested in an authentic laboratory as well as we should also be aware that the rudraksha must be well defined and pure. There should be zero cracks near the central hole and the beads should not be eaten by insects.

Reasons behind do chanting at home

It is believed that chanting is the devotional pathway to reaching the realm. Along with this, it grants tremendous health benefits too. We mostly do chanting in the early morning because as per the shastras – The time of the sunrise is considered as most sattvik because sattva guna is highly active during this time. As a result, the mind is calm and highly focused at this time.

We also follow many steps conducting the chanting at home. The ancient yogis described that these steps have their meaning and importance because they not only prosper us with relaxation but also the way to activate the five senses, such as:

Taking a bath is very beneficial before chanting because it opens the pores of the body and increases blood circulation so that the positive vibration can enter the body easily.

As natural Fibre can absorb energies, so we usually wear neat and clean clothes in chanting, which are mostly made up of cotton or silk. For the same reason, we prefer to wear new or clean clothes during Havana and festivals or go to devotional places, where they can absorb positive energies and give a favourable impact on the body.

It is believed that the bhog also absorbs the positive vibrations of mantras. When we consume it after the chant, it will help to strengthen our chakras and give calmness to the mind.

We also make theertham in a copper or silver vessel, dipped with tulsi leaves in water, and stored for at least eight hours. According to Ayurveda this tulsi water works as medicine and helps to balance the bodily doshas (Vata, pitta, Kapha).

The fragrance of fresh flowers, camphor, and instance sticks also have a strong essence to keep our "sense of smell sense" active and relax the mind. It also purifies the air and can kill the harmful bacteria in the air.

We mostly offer coconut or bananas to deities. The reason is that these fruits are considered to be "Sacred Fruit." Because, to grow a coconut tree, you have to sow the entire coconut itself and the banana tree grows with the sampling.

It is believed that when we ring the bell, they produce a sound, it creates unity in the left and right parts of our brains. Also, the moment we ring the bell, it produces a sharp and enduring sound that lasts for a minimum of 7 seconds in echo mode, it also activates the hearing sense.

By taking certain steps we can nurture a meditative atmosphere at home and increase the positive vibrations and calmness in the environment. If we chant mantras or do meditation in a delightful way we can gain myriad health benefits.

CHAPTER TWENTY-EIGHT

Importance of Surya Arghya

The ancient yogis explained the right way to give Surya Arghya, for getting maximum health benefits: Surya Arghya is to be performed early in the morning during sunrise, wear fresh and clean clothes, take a brass vessel with water for the offering, stand on the balls of your feet and slowly let down a constant trickle of water while looking at the sun through the water flow for 3-5 minutes. The stream of water is not supposed to be broken during the offering. You can recite the Surya mantra along with that. It is believed that this will bring peace and energy to your body in the early morning.

Water can only be offered to the sun when it rises or sets and when the colour of the sun is reddish because only at these two times we can see the sun directly.

Reasons behind offering water to Sun

- At sunrise, the sun rays which are reaching us are slanted. These sun rays are a great source of vitamin D, which is very important for strong and healthy bones.

- When we see the rays of sunlight through the falling water. They get dispersed into seven colours. This spectrum of light enters our body and balances the seven colours in it and energizes the chakras of the body. Secondly, looking at the sun through the stream of water protects our eyes from the harmful sun rays and improves our eyesight too.

- We should be barefoot and stand on the balls of our feet during the offering. This exercise presses the acupressure points that reduce ankle pain and keep our calf muscles healthy.

- Performing the offering of water after taking a bath, leads to better absorption of vitamin D because after a bath the skin gets soft and supple, also with open pores.

- Recitation of mantras helps in concentration and focus.

Thus, offering water to the sun is a very good habit to keep us healthy, so try to include it in your daily routine and get enormous health benefits.

Surya Namaskar Asanas

There is a culture of saluting the sun during the first rays of the sun and performing 12 yoga asanas following it.

Ancient Sages believed that different energies govern different parts of the body. The solar plexus which is located behind the navel is the central point of our body. It is also known as the second brain of the body. Regular practice of Surya Namaskar can enhance the size of the solar plexus.

According to yoga, the Surya Namaskar asanas may help to activate every part of the body. It strengthens the muscles and joints and also provides good flexibility and fitness to people.

CHAPTER TWENTY-NINE

Conventional Procedures

From the older times, our culture and lifestyle are deeply influenced by Ayurvedic norms. These ayurvedic notions might be formed for social welfare and to promote a healthy life. Our ancient eating habits and daily routine beliefs are genuinely concerned with them and unknowingly gain enormous health benefits. Let's look at a few of such practices.

We notice that in old times, all the shopkeepers like cloth merchants, confectioners, jewellers etc. preferred a sitting position at work rather than a standing position. Because at that time most people follow the Ayurveda codes and According to Ayurveda, our bodies are designed in a way that we should not stand for a long time because in this position our legs have to bear our full body weight. Even our blood circulation is also disturbed, as in this state it needs more force to go upward, and our heart requires more strength to pump the blood. Thus, if we work in a standing position for a long time, it can cause sore feet, swelling of the legs, varicose veins, muscle fatigue, low back pain, stiffness in the neck and shoulder, and also can create other health issues. That is why our elders always advise us to do work in a sitting position.

This is also the reason that in older times, people eat food while sitting on the floor as they believe that in this position the digestive juices can excrete properly and let the digestion system work without any disturbance. But if we eat food in a standing position it may speed up the digestion process and food exit the stomach more quickly, resulting in improper digestion. Further, it can create digestion problems such as acid reflux and heartburn, etc.

Similarly, when we drink water in a standing position, this makes the body out of sync with nature, it travels through the system (the liver and digestive tract) faster than it should. Also, it triggers the nervous system, making it alert that some emergency has come up, which makes the body bound to face stress and tension. As a result, the body flushes it out very fast through the kidneys and urinary tract. This, in turn, can also put bones and joints at risk as the water gushes down the body, so you can also experience joint pain. That is why Ayurveda and naturopathy always insist on having food and water in a sitting position.

Ancient sages advised that we should not sleep by keeping our heads in the south direction. They may have known that the earth and the human body both have magnetic fields of their own. Magnetic fields on the earth concentrate on the north and the South Poles. India lies in the northern hemisphere and our ancestors were also aware of it. Hence, they preferred to sleep with their head facing the south. We all know that opposite poles attract. Therefore, they were scientifically correct. When we sleep by keeping our heads in the south direction, gradually our body's magnetic field conflicts with the magnetic field of the earth. As a result, this may cause fluctuation in blood pressure and our heart has to work harder to maintain balance.

Secondly, our blood contains a lot of iron content. Thus when we sleep facing north, the magnetic pull of the direction triggers iron to get accumulated in the brain. This can be the reason why many people complain of getting a headache when they wake up.

But it is important to note that these effects are very minor daily and they will become prominent only then when we do it consistently. But elderly people and heart patients might get more affected than others.

Our elders always advised that when we wake up in the morning, we should chant some mantras and then get up from bed. Somewhere the reason can be, as when we rise swiftly, then this change in position of the body from horizontal to vertical, a gravitational force pulls blood towards our feet which can increase the chances of a heart attack. But if we chant the mantras, this way we can spend some time on it, in the meantime our body can regulate its blood circulation and our day starts with positive vibrations.

We have ever seen that ancient sages either tie the Shikha on the head or cover the head with cloth because they believed that it is the place of Brahmadhara (crown chakra) where the Sushumna Nadi arrives from the lower part of the body and also it is considered as the centre of wisdom. Sushrut rishi, the foremost surgeon of Ayurveda, describes the master sensitive spot on the head as Adhipati Marma(centre of the head), where there is a nexus of all nerves. So, the ancient yogis covered this place with knotted hair to protect this spot and also conserve the subtle energy known as Ojas.

When a new baby is born, usually our elders store a part of the umbilical cord in a capsule made of copper. As it is believed that this umbilical cord tissue is rich in stem cells. Stem cells are immature cells that can both reproduce themselves and have the potential to turn into other types of cells. They are also more easily accepted by the body than the stem cells of bone marrow. That is why in recent years, many people preserve it in cord blood banks so that in an emergency, it can help in treating the diseases.

We usually keep fasting during the changing seasons (April and October) but maybe we don't know that they are loaded with health benefits. As the eating habits of both the seasons (summer and winter) are quite different from each other. Thereby, we notice that the change of season also brings along with illness and diseases. So to get rid of them, if we keep fasting for several days, it might help to give enough time to the body to adjust and prepare itself for the changing season. According to Ayurveda, when we opt for a sattvic diet, it strengthens the body and minds very effectively because when we consume a variety of fruits and nutritious food, our immunity increases as the antioxidants present in these foods help to remove harmful free radicals and toxins from the body. We also replace table salt with sendha namak during these days because it aids digestion, boosts immunity, regulates blood pressure, and keeps the body active throughout the day. Furthermore, when our body is in an alkaline state (during fast) and if we chant mantras then it will be more effective. This may be the reason we feel light after chanting during fast.

Similarly, our ancestors prohibit us to consume milk during the monsoon because According to Ayurveda: In these months (July, and August) the Vata (gas) component of the body tends to be high. So, a person must avoid food that increases the Vata component. Green leafy vegetables contain higher amounts of data in them and during the rainy season, the cattle eat lots of grass, and hence their milk is high in Vata. For this reason, consuming milk is prohibited in Vedas during the Shravan month. If you have noticed that this is the time when we often suffer Vata dominant diseases like bloating, muscle stiffness, joint pain, etc, these diseases flourish due to an imbalance in 'Vata Pitta and Kapha in the body. That is why Ayurveda advises us to avoid consuming dairy products in monsoon months.

Mostly our meals start with spice and end with some sweetness. According to Ayurveda, spice activates the digestive juices and acids to boost our digestive system efficiently. As sweets contain carbohydrates that slow down the digestive process. Secondly, the intake of sugar enhances the absorption of amino acid tryptophan which is linked with the feeling of fullness. Therefore, sweets are always served at the end of meals so that the food can be digested properly.

There is a tradition that when someone is going out for important work (exam, deals, meetings, etc.) they should eat a combination of curd and sugar before leaving home. According to Ayurveda, this combination of curd and sugar tends to make you feel calm. Because the consumption of curd provides a cooling effect on the stomach and the sugar provides instant glucose, so the person feels more energetic. Maybe, for this reason, ancestors linked it to good luck because they knew that when we remain calm and cool, we can focus on work more effectively.

Thus, there are plenty of traditions that we follow unknowingly, for sure our wise ancestors set them for us for gaining better mental and physical health.

Human Body

The human body is one of the most complicated living forms on earth. But surprisingly, we are unaware of how mysterious a body we have. We must be thankful for medical science and the great researchers who have put their hard efforts and revealed the amazing facts about our bodies which have astonished us.

CHAPTER THIRTY

Interesting Facts about Human Body

No matter how much we have known about our body, still, our bio-machine is full of surprises. In the end, let's freshen up with some interesting features that make our body special:

- The human body contains nearly 100 trillion cells and interestingly 50,000 cells in your body die and were replaced by now while you were reading this sentence. More of that every second our body produces 25 million new cells. That means in 15 seconds, we will have produced more cells than there are people in the United States.

- A large amount of the dust in our home is our dead skin. As humans shed about 600,000 particles of skin every hour. It means approximately that we lose about 4 kg of skin cells every year.

- There are anywhere between 60,000–100,000 miles long of blood vessels in the human body. Just think, if they are taken out and laid end to end, they would be long enough to travel around the world more than 3 times, as the earth is: 24,873.6 miles [according to NASA].

- Capillaries: the body's smallest blood vessels are so small that it takes 10 of them side by side to equal the thickness of one strand of human hair.

- The heart is supposed to be the strongest muscle in the body which beats approximately 100,000 times per day.

- More of that in one year, a human heart would pump enough blood to fill an Olympic size pool.

- Interestingly, human blood has the same ratio of salt in it as the ocean does.

- The highest blood flow is in the kidneys. On average, each day the kidney processes about 500 gallons of blood to filter out.

- At birth, there are 14 billion cells in the human brain. After 25 years the number of cells falls by 10,000 every day.

- The human brain contains about 100 billion neurons.

- The brain uses 20% of oxygen and blood in the body and Only 5 minutes without oxygen can lead to brain damage.

- If we smoothed out all the wrinkles in our brain it would lay flat the size of a Pillowcase.

- The human brain has a memory capacity that is the equivalent of more than four terabytes on a hard drive.

- Nerve impulses in the human body move at a speed of about 90m/s or 274km/h.

- Approximately, 100,000 chemical reactions occur in the human brain every second.

- When we touch something the signal travels through the nerve to the brain at a speed of 124 mph.

- More of that the brain generates between 12-25 watts of electricity, which is enough to power a low-watt voltage light bulb.

- We lose 80% of our body heat from the head. That is why we should always cover our head with a cloth under the sun's rays so that it can protect from heating up and remain cool down.

- A feeling of thirst occurs when our body water loss is equal to 1% of our body weight. The loss of more than 5% can cause fainting and more than 10% causes death from dehydration.

- Our nose and ears continue growing throughout our entire life.

- Teeth are considered part of the skeletal system but are not counted as bones. Teeth are the only part of the human body that cannot heal themselves.

- Human teeth are just as strong as shark teeth.

- Our tongue is made up of eight interwoven muscles, similar in structure to an elephant's trunk or an octopus's tentacle.

- As well as having unique fingerprints, humans also have unique tongue prints.

- There are about ten thousand taste buds on the human tongue and in general girls have more taste buds than boys.

- The average person produces enough saliva in their lifetime to fill two swimming pools. As our mouth produces about one litre of saliva each day.

- There are approximately 40,000 bacteria in the human mouth.
- The nose can recognize approximately a trillion different scents.
- A sneeze blows air out of our nose at 100 miles per hour.
- An adult person performs around 23,000 inhalations and exhalations a day, and breaths in around 11,000 litres of air every day.
- Lungs are the only organs in the body that floats.
- There are more than 100 different viruses that cause a cold.
- Extraocular muscles in the eye are the body's fastest muscles. They allow both of our eyes to flick in the same direction in a single 50-millisecond movement.
- The cornea is the only part of the body with no blood supply, it gets its oxygen directly from the air.
- An eyelash lives for about 150 days before it falls out.
- On average, we will blink approximately 4200,000 times in a single year.
- If the human eye is a digital camera, it would have 576 megapixels.
- More of that, the human eye can differentiate approximately 10 million different colours.
- Beards are the fastest-growing hair on the human body. If the average man never trimmed his beard it would grow to nearly 30 feet long in his lifetime.

- Fingernails and hair are made out of the same substance; Keratin.
- Our liver performs more than 200 different functions in the body. It is the only organ in the body with the ability to regenerate.
- Babies don't shed tears until they are at least one month old.
- We can't breathe and swallow at the same time, but a newborn child can breathe and swallow at the same time for 7 months.
- The human body has 650 muscles (don't count cardiac and smooth muscles) and we use 200 muscles to take a single step forward.
- The muscle that can generate the most power is our Jaw muscle.
- 50% of our hand strength comes from our little fingers.
- Thumbs have their pulse.
- Bones are as strong as steel.
- Everyone has unique kneecaps that can be used as biometrics.
- Babies are born without kneecaps as knee joints are made out of cartilage and it turns into bones between the age of two -six.
- The spinal disc core is composed of a large volume of water therefore dehydration could lead to back pain.
- An average-sized man eats about 33 tons of food in his/her lifetime, which is about the weight of 'Six Elephants.'

- The average human body contains- Enough Sulphur to kill all the fleas on the average dog. Enough Carbon to make 900 pencils, Enough Iron to make a nail 2.5 cm long, Enough Potassium to fire a toy cannon, Enough Fat to make seven bars of soaps Enough Water to fill 50 litres barrel.

- At least 700 enzymes are active in the human body.

- The average person has 67 different species of bacteria in their belly button.

- The total weight of the bacteria in the human body is 2 kg.

- We carry on average about four pounds of bacteria around our body. Only 1% of bacteria can result in the human body becoming ill.

- Our gastro-internal system is often referred to as the 'second brain' as it is the only organ with an independent nervous system, comprising 100 million neurons embedded in the gut wall. That is why, when our brain is not able to communicate with our gut (paralyzed or in coma etc.) neurons in our gut wall would still be able to transmit the necessary information on its own.

- Humans are the only ones that enjoy spicy food.

- We can't taste food without saliva.

- Aeroplane food tastes bad because of low humidity and low air pressure.

- Butterflies in the stomach are real and they are caused by adrenaline.

- Kidney stones are more common in summer because hot weather leads to dehydration which causes more kidney stones.

- There are about 1.15 million nephrons in your kidney. If they stretch out from end to end they are about 5 miles (8 km) long.

- In some cases, if a child is born without one kidney, the other one will grow and weigh the same as two kidneys put together.

- The spine has exceptional memory. Once you do make a habit of good posture, your spine will remember it.

- Each hair strand has its muscle, nerve, and blood supply.

- More of that, a strand of healthy hair is stronger than a copper wire with the same diameter.

- Also, hair contains information about everything that has been in your bloodstreams such as medicine, drugs, minerals, and vitamins. The only thing that can't be identified by hair is gender.

- Interestingly In humans, there are about 28,000 to 30,000 genes in each cell and nearly 12,000 to 13,000 genes in each of the chromosomes.

- Every human being shares about 99% of their DNA with every other human.

- If you put all the DNA molecules in your body end to end, the DNA would reach from the earth to the Sun.

- We share,

  - 98.7% of our DNA with Chimpanzees,

  - 85% of our DNA with Mouse,
  - 40% of our DNA with butterflies,
  - 41% of our DNA is Banana.

- Biologists believe that there is a limit to how long we can live(max.125 years), no matter how good our living conditions are, as ageing itself might be connected to the DNA damage that can't be reversed.

- The average moderately active person takes around 5000 steps /day and maintains it till 70 years of age, he walks the equivalent of 3 times around the world.

- Vitamin B1 is essential to producing the brain chemical acetylcholine, which is needed for concentrating and storing memories.

- Vitamin D is the only vitamin that is also a hormone and that deficiency can lead to numerous mental diseases.

- The sense of smell connects to the part of the brain that also controls emotions and memories. This is why smells often evoke strong memories.

- A small area in the brain called the amygdala is responsible for our ability to read someone else's face for clues to how they are feeling.

- Humans grow faster at night because the pituitary gland releases a growth hormone at night while a person sleeps.

- The average number of thoughts that humans are believed to experience each day is 70,000.

- Alcohol doesn't make you forget anything when you get blackout drunk, but the brain temporarily loses the ability to create memories.

- The first 3 seconds you wake up, you will not remember anything.

- You can die from fear because the body releases a big amount of adrenaline which can be toxic in high amounts.

- Laughing at a joke is no simple task as it requires activity in five different areas of the brain.

- The first sense to develop while in the uterus is the sense of touch. The lips and cheeks can experience touch at about 8 weeks and the rest of the body around 12 weeks.

- Smaller fingers have a better sense of touch because they have more sense receptors packed together in small areas.

- Cracking the fingers is a bad habit - because when we crack our knuckles, we are pulling our joints apart. This stretch causes air bubbles to form in the fluid which eventually pops creating that familiar sound. But we should not practice it frequently because it can lead to hand swelling, weaken the grip and make it easier for our joints to crack.

- Playing Video games can have some good side effects on kids too as video games give kids a chance to settle down their negative emotions, and also to face and defeat scary things. Even playing video games improves the alertness of the brain and the presence of the mind.

- Our mind spends about 70% of its time replaying memories and creating scenarios of perfect moments.

- Cuddling releases natural pain killer oxytocin. It decreases headaches significantly.

- It is stated that, if you sob out of happiness, the first tear will come from the right eye, but if you cry out of sorrow it will come from the left.

- A plant can grow inside the human body as a Fir tree (measuring 5 cm) has been found growing inside a man's lung by a Russian Surgeon, who was operating on him for suspected cancer.

- We can't imagine that the colour of blood in the human body can be green but in fact, Sulfhemoglobinemia is a rare condition that can cause human blood to turn "Green."

Our human body is full of wonders, some are disclosed, some have been proven but we don't know how many are remaining.

Afterword

We make mistakes no matter how much we know. Misconceptions become our daily routine and we have habits that harm us instead of curing us. Even when we are introduced to natural science like Yoga and Ayurveda, we follow things blindly without actually knowing the facts. I have tried my best to capture many misconceptions about these daily health routines but there is much more to it than the content of this book.

If you enjoyed reading this book, please take a few moments to write a review of it. You can also connect with me through naturopath.geetagupta@gmail.com.

I hope we meet again between the pages of another book. Thank you!

9 798887 338354

Printed by Libri Plureos GmbH in Hamburg,
Germany